Do You Know Dinos?

IGUANODON

Professor Michael J Benton – d̶i̶ ̶ ̶ ̶ ̶ ̶ ̶a̶nt
Valerie Wilding – educational advisor
Ben Newth – researcher

Scholastic Children's Books,
Euston House, 24 Eversholt Street,
London NW1 1DB, UK

A division of Scholastic Ltd
London ~ New York ~ Toronto ~ Sydney ~ Auckland
Mexico City ~ New Delhi ~ Hong Kong

First published in the UK by Scholastic Ltd, 2003
(as *Now You Know: Iguanodon – the dinosaur with the fat bottom*)
This edition published 2010

ISBN 978 1407 11463 7

Printed in the UK by CPI Bookmarque, Croydon, CR0 4TD

2 4 6 8 10 9 7 5 3 1

Contents

Introduction **5**

Iguanodon has a bite to eat **6**

Iguanodon gets into a fight **22**

Iguanodon lays some eggs **40**

Iguanodon is discovered **50**

Dino News! **64**

Dinner in a dino **68**

Quizzes! **72**

Index **79**

Introduction

Do you know
how to talk dino? It's
easier to say dino names in bits:

Ig-wah-nerd-on

Say it slowly, then say it faster. Now
you'll remember how to say Iguanodon!

Iguanodon has a bite to eat

A lot of dinosaurs had fat bottoms.
Iguanodon may not have had the fattest
bottom of all, but have
a look:

Iguanodon
bottom

Your
bottom

It is big, isn't it?

Do you know why Iguanodon needed such a fat bottom?

Was it nice to sit on?

Oof!

Was it good for bumping other dinosaurs out of the way?

Was it because Iguanodon was a greedy dinosaur?

Nobody can say for sure.

The world looked different when Iguanodon was alive. Some of the creatures it saw are still around today, like turtles, lizards, snakes, fish – even beetles and spiders.

But there were lots of other dinosaurs, too! Iguanodon could look up to see a huge pterosaur (ter-oh-sore) flying across the sky.

Or an enormous plesiosaur (please-ee-oh-sore) swimming in the sea.

Dinosaurs came in all shapes and sizes, from little Hypsilophodon (hip-sil-oaf-oh-don), to absolutely enormous Brachiosaurus (brack-ee-oh-sore-us).

There were huge forests with very tall trees. The biggest dinosaurs were so big, they ripped up whole trees for food! And when the sun shone on the forest floor, smaller plants started to grow.

Iguanodon probably saw some of the
first flowers *ever* ...

… and ate them!

Yes, Iguanodon was a vegetarian dinosaur. It didn't eat meat.

Iguanodon had to make do with leaves, ferns, plants, even small trees – and maybe some fruits and seeds if it was lucky!

So the flowers made a tasty change!

The leaves that grew millions of years ago were tough. Really tough. Iguanodon probably had lots of tummy aches.

RRRUMBLE

Chomp

1 Iguanodon needed a big tummy to cope with all the food it ate.

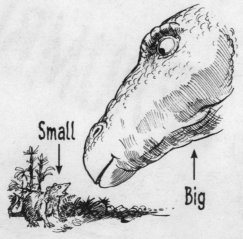

Small

Big

2 Because it had a big tummy it was a big dinosaur.

3 And because it was a big dinosaur, it had to keep eating nearly all the time.

4 It needed a big, fat bottom to balance that big, fat tummy!

Parp!

To get down to some serious eating,
Iguanodon had to get comfortable. It
rested on its chunky back legs and used
its stiff, straight tail to prop itself up
(a bit like having a stool
stuck to your bottom!).

Instead of front teeth it had a sort
of beak. The beak nipped off the tasty

green leaves and shoots, leaving behind the twiggy bits. Iguanodon chewed the greens with its back teeth and swallowed them into that enormous tum.

Beak

Scientists think dinosaur teeth are really exciting. Teeth tell them all sorts of things about a dinosaur.

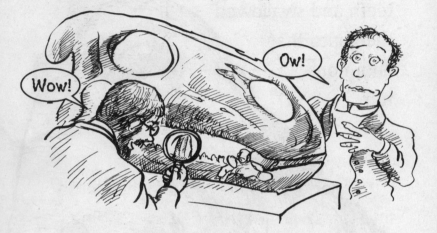

They know Iguanodon was a vegetarian because its teeth weren't strong enough to cut into meat.

Iguanodon's teeth looked like this:

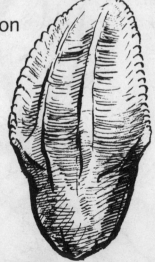

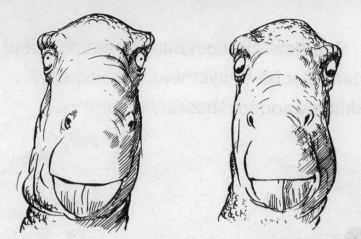

They were good for chewing, not for ripping other animals to bits!

Iguanodon's top jaw slid from side to side to make it easier to chew. Sliding jaws helped grind up food and kept Ig's teeth nice and sharp, too. Which is quite clever really!

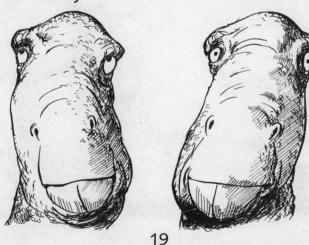

Bad news: a dinosaur that ate a lot had to poo a lot. Maybe four times a day! A good use for that fat bottom!

Good news: the poos didn't smell as bad as you think. And they were good for the plants!

Seeds that Iguanodon ate with its dinner ...

Seeds

... came out again when it pooed ...

... so more plants grew.

Poo

Iguanodon gets into a fight

Seeing Iguanodon chomping its way through the forest would be scary, wouldn't it? Iguanodon wouldn't hurt you, though … as long as you kept out of the way! And that's just what a lot of creatures did.

They kept out of Iguanodon's way
because it *looked* big and scary. Another
good reason for having a fat bottom!
Iguanodon could use it – and the rest of
its body – to frighten
other animals.

Sometimes Iguanodon did get nasty. It could protect itself with the help of its amazing hands. Each one was like a hand and a foot all in one! And they were a bit different from yours. Have a look:

Iguanodon hand

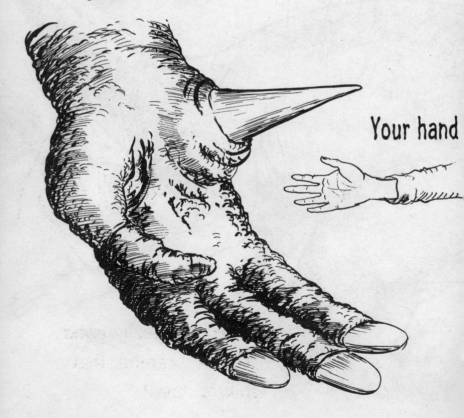

Your hand

What could you do if your hands looked like this?

• A handstand – easy!

• Open a can with your thumb!

• Have a really good scratch – careful, that spike's sharp!

The three middle fingers on Iguanodon's hand worked more like toes:

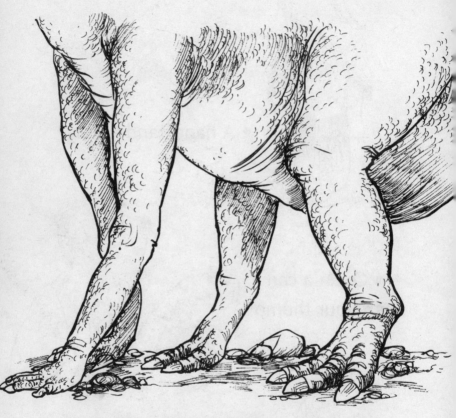

Iguanodon walked and ran on its legs, but it could use its arms too, for standing or resting. Sometimes it walked on all fours, especially when it was looking for food.

Standing still

Walking on all fours

Running

Iguanodon's bendy little finger could hold on to twigs and things as it ate.

And then there was the spike! It was great for breaking open seed pods and fruits, but there was another good use for it …

... to swipe at enemies!

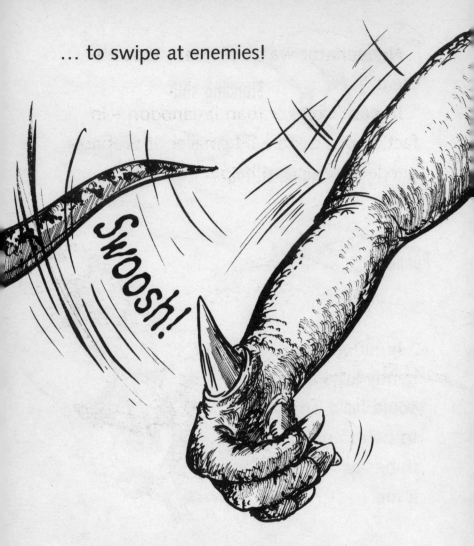

Swoosh!

Even though Iguanodon was huge, some other dinos thought it might be a tasty meal. Neovenator (knee-oh-venner-tor) was one of them.

Neovenator was a dinosaur that ate meat.

It wasn't bigger than Iguanodon – in fact, it was quite a bit smaller. It probably needed a friend to help it attack.

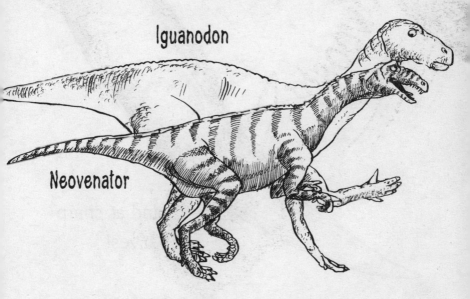

Iguanodon

Neovenator

Neovenator ran on two legs, like Iguanodon. It also had a long tail, like Iguanodon. But its bottom wasn't nearly so fat and …

… Neovenator had great big legs, so it could run even faster than you. It had nasty, sharp claws on its fingers.

And you wouldn't want to go near those teeth!

They were this big …

… and as sharp as knives!

Neovenator would jump out at Iguanodon, jaws open, ready to bite! It would try to use its claws to stop Iguanodon running away.

But Iguanodon could fight back. Jabbing its thumb spike into Neovenator's eye or throat. Nasty!

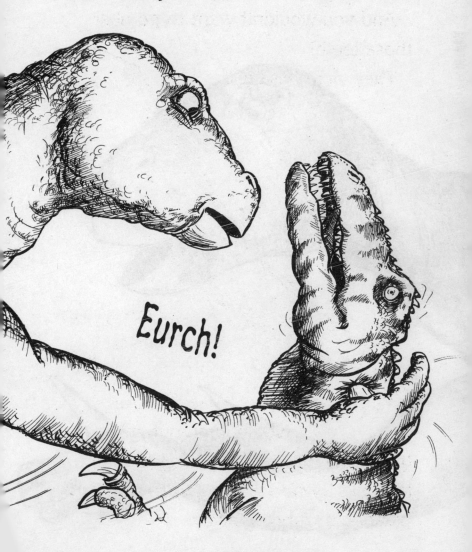

Eurch!

Then there was Baryonyx (barry-on-ics).
Some scientists found a Baryonyx
skeleton near some Iguanodon bones.

They thought Baryonyx liked to hunt and eat Iguanodons.

Baryonyx had jaws a bit like a crocodile. It walked on two legs and had a huge hook on its hand. The hook was sharp and deadly. An easy match for Iguanodon's thumb spike.

So did Baryonyx and Iguanodon fight?
Other scientists say this is rubbish.
Baryonyx only ate Iguanodons that were
already dead. This means Baryonyx was
a "scavenger", not a killer.

The scientists think Baryonyx lived near water. Its big hands, its claws and even its crocodile mouth were just right for catching fish.

Fishing was a lot easier than fighting Iguanodon, even though Baryonyx couldn't actually swim!

Being a great big Iguanodon wasn't enough to scare off all small dinos.

Deinonychus (die-none-eek-us) had quite a long tail, but it wasn't much taller than you. And you wouldn't want to get too close! Deinonychus definitely *wasn't* friendly!

It hunted in a gang with four or five others. Together, they could hunt for bigger dinosaurs. Deinonychus had sharp teeth and killer claws, too. The nastiest claw of all was ...

... on its foot.

Ouch!

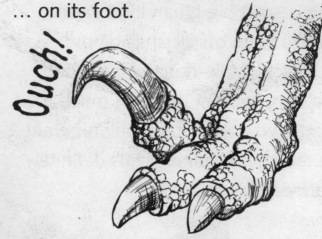

The Deinonychus gang jumped on
Iguanodon. Then, balancing on one leg,
they used the other to jab their killer toe
claws into Iguanodon's tum.

38

Iguanodon fought back
by whacking them away
with its huge tail ...

... kicking its big
back legs ...

Hurray!

... or using its fat bottom – to squash
them!

39

Iguanodon lays some eggs

Life for Iguanodons wasn't all eating and fighting. They had babies, too!

No one has ever seen an Iguanodon egg, but scientists think the mum laid them in a nest. Iguanodon was a bit big to nest up a tree! Instead it used its arms to dig a nest from soft, dry earth. It looked like this...

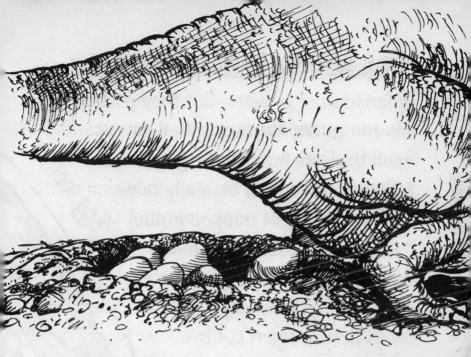

… and held 20 or 30 eggs. (Imagine all those brothers and sisters!) But the eggs were a tasty treat for lizards and small, hungry dinosaurs. So laying lots of eggs meant at least a few would hatch and survive.

Slurp!

Nobody knows exactly what size Iguanodon eggs were, but they probably weren't as big as you think. Big eggs need thick shells. If the egg was really big, the shell would be really thick. A baby might get trapped inside!

Iguanodon babies had teeth before they hatched. They even had a special egg tooth to help them cut the eggshell. They needed the tooth because, even though the egg wasn't huge, its shell was still this thick:

Egg tooth

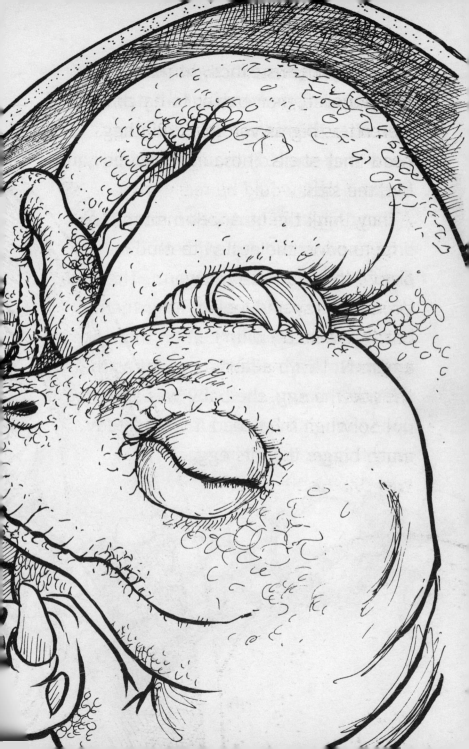

At first, scientists thought that dinosaurs left their babies to hatch and look after themselves. But now they know that some dinosaurs really did care for their kids.

They think the Iguanodon mum took time to cover the nest with mud or plants, to keep the eggs warm. Then she stayed nearby and looked after them, but she probably didn't sit on them like a hen. Not with a bottom as fat as that!

Inside the egg, the baby was all curled up! So when it hatched it was already much bigger than its egg.

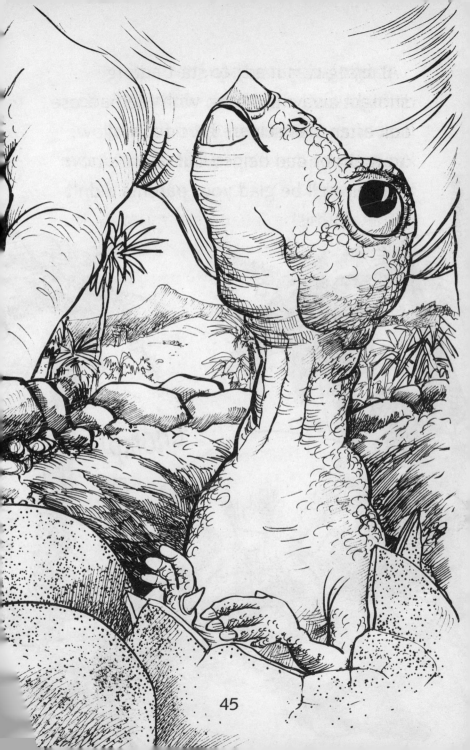

Baby Ig was ready to start eating straight away. But even with teeth, those leaves and ferns were hard to swallow. So mum or dad helped out. Here's how – and you'll be glad your parents didn't do this!

Chomp!

Mum or dad chewed some tough old leaves, and swallowed them down.
Then they sicked them up again.
Hey presto! Baby food!
Sounds disgusting, doesn't it? But birds still do this today.

Chomp!

Like most babies, baby Ig had a big head and big eyes. If these important body parts are big when the baby hatches, they don't have to grow much more. If they don't have to grow much, there's less that can go wrong with them. The baby has a better chance of growing up healthy and strong.

And the big eyes helped in another way, too. They made baby Ig's mum and dad want to look after it, because they thought their baby looked *gorgeous*.

Ahhhh!

Iguanodon is discovered

Dinosaurs lived and died long before there were people.

So scientists only found out about them by looking at fossils. Fossils are bones or traces of dinosaurs, like a footprint or a tail trail, that have turned to rock over millions of years.

People didn't always know what fossils were. The first scientists to discover fossilized dinosaur bones found that not many people believed them!

An English Doctor, called Gideon Mantell, discovered Iguanodon over 150 years ago. Dr Mantell's hobby was fossil hunting. He spent all his spare time searching in the woods near his home.

One day he and his wife, Mary, came across a different sort of fossil. It looked like a tooth! A very strange tooth. He knew it belonged to a very unusual creature.

Very interesting.

Dr Mantell thought the tooth came from some sort of giant lizard. But other scientists laughed at him. They said the tooth was from:

An elephant!

A rhinoceros!

A big fish!

Dr Mantell set out to prove the scientists wrong.

He searched through drawers and drawers of lizard and snake skeletons. Creepy!

And he found something! His fossil tooth was just like the tooth of an iguana. That's a modern type of lizard.

But the fossil tooth was 20 times bigger. This was quite some lizard!

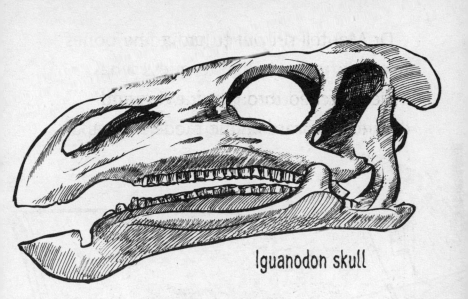

Iguanodon skull

Iguana skull

Dr Mantell called the creature
Iguanodon. Which means "iguana
tooth". And he wrote about it, saying
that giant reptiles once walked the
forests of southern England.

People stopped laughing and started
to listen to him.

Dr Mantell only ever had a few bones to work from. He had to guess what his creature looked like. He thought Iguanodon was like the modern iguana:

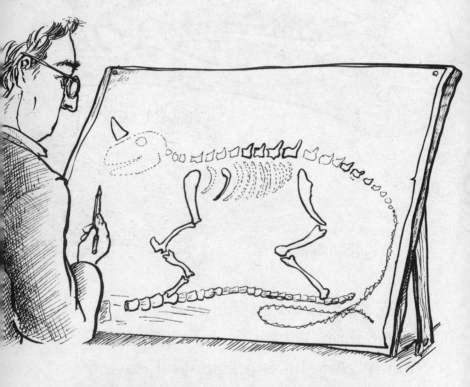

Other scientists had different ideas. They thought the creature was more like a rhinoceros, with four huge legs and a very fat bottom!

Can you see what happened to the
thumb spike? They all put it on the end
of Iguanodon's nose!

Sadly, Mantell was already dead when miners in Belgium dug up some old bones. They were huge bones, and there were so many of them, the miners called in dino expert Louis Dollo.

There wasn't just one skeleton. There were more than 30 Iguanodon skeletons buried in the mine! There were fossils of other creatures and plants, too!

It was an amazing discovery. Dollo studied the different sorts of fossils for the rest of his long life. He started to work out how Iguanodon lived.

When Dollo put the bones together, the skeletons looked like this:

He thought Iguanodon was more like a kangaroo than a rhinoceros!

And Dollo found out loads about Iguanodon. Lots of the things he discovered are things you've read about in this book:
- It definitely walked on two legs.
- Its arms were used for grasping food.
- It had *two* spikes, one on each thumb!

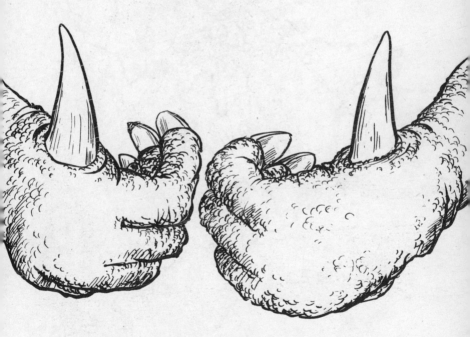

Scientists are finding out new dinosaur facts all the time.

Today, Iguanodon looks different again! Scientists say it had a stiff tail. It held its tail up to balance the rest of its body. It wasn't as big or heavy as early scientists thought, and its bottom wasn't quite so fat!

Iguanodon find ◉
Iguanodon relative find ◼

Fossils of Iguanodon and its relatives have been found all over the world. We know more about Iguanodon than most other dinosaurs. That might just prove that Iguanodon was the most successful dinosaur EVER!

DINONEWS

December 2008

STOP PRESS!
WORLD'S BIGGEST DINO DIG

It's in China, near a place named Zhucheng (but you can call it Dinosaur City, everyone else does). Dinosaur fossils have been found in over 30 sites close to the city. The first finds were made over 40 years ago, when people started mining for oil.

But this time it's really BIG news. In less than a year, researchers have found over 7,000 bones! The bones belong to different types of dinos. And scientists think they might help them to solve a very important mystery ... why the dinosaurs died out.

IGUANODON'S LONG LOST COUSIN

If you think scientists know all the dinosaurs that ever lived, think again!

Dino digs have been big news in Europe and the US for well over 100 years. But, in the last 30 years, dino fever has spread around the world.

In South America, meat-eating dinosaurs, and huge sauropods, like Diplodocus, have already been found. Now, a dino that's a bit like Iguanodon has been discovered there too.

Big digs are happening in Mongolia, Russia and even Antarctica. Who knows what they'll dig up next!

BOY'S BRILLIANT BEACH FIND

AN EIGHT-YEAR-OLD SCHOOLBOY MADE A BRILLIANT DISCOVERY ON A BEACH IN YORKSHIRE.

Rhys Nichols was amazed when he saw some fossilized footprints in the rock.

Experts were impressed – the footprints were in fantastic condition! But Rhys was a bit disappointed when they told him that the prints only belonged to a diddy dino. It probably wasn't much bigger than Rhys! And it wasn't a terrifying meat-eater, like T.rex. It was a veggie, like Iguanodon.

WHAT NEXT FOR IGUANODON?

It's hard to think there's a future for a dinosaur that died out millions of years ago, but Iguanodon has already made a comeback. Clever scientists have made a sheep-sized, iguanodon-shaped robot that can walk about without bumping into things. They're working on improvements though, as so far robot Ig can only walk very, very slowly…

Dinner in a dino

When Gideon Mantell died, Victoria was still the queen of England. And Victorians carried on being crazy about dinos. They were desperate to see what these new creatures really looked like.

A man called Waterhouse Hawkins was asked to make some models. He invited dinosaur expert, Richard Owen, to advise him.

The models were made from bricks, tiles, cement, stone and iron. They were massive, amazing, life-sized models. Hawkins made three dinosaurs all together. Iguanodon was one of them.

Before big Ig was finished, the two men invited twenty-one VIPs for a New Year's Eve party – in its tum! They sat at tables inside the monster and enjoyed an eight-course meal with lots of wine.

Newspapers sent journalists to scribble reports and artists to draw pictures of the scene.

The guests ended their dinner with a song:

The jolly old beast
Is not deceased*
There's life in him again!
Roar!!

They kept on singing and roaring as they wobbled off home.

*Deceased is another word for "dead".

It was a good job Gideon Mantell wasn't there. Before he died he'd worked out that Iguanodon probably walked on two legs, not four. He might have spoiled the party! Dinner in a *two*-legged dino would have been very wobbly indeed.

Di-yes/Di-no quiz

You've read the book, so these puzzles will be eea-sy! Just answer "di-yes" or "di-no" to each of these sentences:

1 Iguanodon was a ferocious, meat-eating dinosaur. Di-yes/Di-no
2 Iguanodon had a thumb spike on its bottom. Di-yes/Di-no
3 Iguanodon had a beak. Di-yes/Di-no
4 Deinonychus was smaller than Iguanodon, but it wasn't too scared to attack the bigger dino. Di-yes/Di-no
5 Mum Iguanodon sicked up food for baby Ig. Di-yes/Di-no
6 Iguanodon got its name because Gideon Mantell, who discovered it, thought Ig looked like a rhinoceros. Di-yes/Di-no

Answers

1 Di-no it wasn't! (See pages 12–13)
2 Di-no it didn't! (See pages 27–28)
3 Di-yes it did! (See page 17)
4 Di-yes, that's true. (See pages 37–39)
5 Oh, di-yes, that's true! (See page 47)
6 Oh, di-no it didn't. (See page 53)
7 Di-no it wasn't! (See page 21)
8 Di-yes, that's right. (See pages 34–35)
9 Yikes, di-no she didn't! (See page 44)
10 Di-yes, it was. (See pages 56–58)

7 Iguanodon poo was really smelly.
Di-yes/Di-no
8 A Baryonyx was just as happy to
eat a tasty fish as it was tucking in to
Iguanodon meat. Di-yes/Di-no
9 Iguanodon Mum kept her eggs warm
by sitting on her nest. Di-yes/Di-no
10 The first complete Iguanodon
skeleton was only found after Gideon
Mantell was dead. Di-yes/Di-no

How well do you know dinos?

Show off your dino know-how. Match each picture with a fact and a name. Can you get them all right?

Deinonychus   **Iguanodon**
Baryonyx   **Plesiosaur**
Hypsilophodon   **Brachiosaurus**
Neovenator   **Pterosaur**

The one with the fat bottom.
A huge, ancient sea creature.
A giant flying reptile.
A dinky little dino.
One of the biggest dinos ever!
A speedy dino with teeth as sharp as knives.
This dino was good at fishing.
An unfriendly dino with weapons on its toes.

Answers

Iguanodon
The one with the fat bottom.

Plesiosaur
A huge, ancient sea creature.

Pterosaur
A giant flying reptile.

Hypsilophodon
A dinky little dino.

Brachiosaurus
One of the biggest dinos.

Deinonychus
A speedy dino with teeth sharp as knives.

Baryonyx
This dino was good at fishing.

Neovenator
An unfriendly dino with weapons on its toes.

Dinosearch

D	R	A	Z	I	L	T	N	A	I	G	N	I
M	H	U	T	H	E	F	R	L	U	R	Y	G
Z	I	M	J	Y	A	O	N	G	E	T	Q	U
P	N	I	F	T	E	V	X	F	E	P	L	A
R	O	O	R	A	G	N	A	K	T	K	E	N
A	C	P	M	F	E	L	I	T	P	E	R	O
J	E	R	A	T	D	P	T	I	R	V	A	D
K	R	L	S	R	S	L	D	F	A	J	C	O
B	O	V	T	B	O	T	T	O	M	X	O	N
I	S	O	M	A	N	T	E	L	L	R	L	K
G	T	U	B	L	C	R	O	S	P	Y	L	R
E	H	T	O	O	T	G	G	E	R	F	O	A
T	S	N	A	L	R	P	I	T	Q	U	D	L

There are twelve words, or pairs of words, hidden in this Dinosearch. Look at the list below and see if you can find them all. It's not easy! They might be written up, down, backwards, forwards or diagonally.

BOTTOM	**IGUANODON**
DOLLO	KANGAROO
EGG TOOTH	**MANTELL**
FAT	REPTILE
FERN	**RHINOCEROS**
GIANT LIZARD	THUMB SPIKE

Answers

Did you find them all?

D	R	A	Z	I	L	T	N	A	I	G	N	I
M	H	U	T	H	E	F	R	L	U	R	Y	G
Z	I	M	J	Y	A	O	N	G	E	T	Q	U
P	N	I	F	T	E	V	X	F	E	P	L	A
R	O	O	R	A	G	N	A	K	T	K	E	N
A	C	P	M	F	E	L	I	T	P	E	R	O
J	E	R	A	T	D	P	T	I	R	V	A	D
K	R	L	S	R	S	L	D	F	A	J	C	O
B	O	V	T	B	O	T	T	O	M	X	O	N
I	S	O	M	A	N	T	E	L	L	R	L	K
G	T	U	B	L	C	R	O	S	P	Y	L	R
E	H	T	O	O	T	G	G	E	R	F	O	A
T	S	N	A	L	R	P	I	T	Q	U	D	L

78

Index

arms 26, 61

babies 40, 42, 44, 46–8, 72
Baryonyx 32, 34–5, 73–4
beak 16–17, 72
birds 47
bottom 6–7, 15, 20, 23, 29, 39, 44, 56–7, 62, 75–6
Brachiosaurus 10, 74

Deinonychus 37–8, 72, 74
Dinosaur City 64
Diplodocus 65
Dollo, Louis 58, 60–1

eating 12, 14–16, 33, 46, 72–3
eggs 40–2, 73
eyes 48

fighting 22, 31, 39
fossils 50–4, 58, 63–4, 67

hands 24–6, 35
Hawkins, Waterhouse 68
Hypsilophodon 10, 74

jaws 19, 30, 33

legs 16, 26, 29–30, 33, 38–9, 56, 61, 70

Mantell, Gideon 52–6, 58, 68, 70, 72–3

Neovenator 28–30, 74
nests 40, 44, 73
Nichols, Rhys 67

Owen, Richard 68

plants 10, 12, 21, 44, 58
Plesiosaur 9, 74
poo 20–1, 73
Pterosaur 9, 74

robots 66

sauropods 65
scavengers 34
scientists 32, 34–5, 40, 44, 50–1, 53–4, 56, 61–2, 64–6
skeletons 32, 54, 58, 60, 73
spikes 25, 27, 31, 33, 57, 61, 72

T.rex 67
tail 16, 29, 37, 39, 50, 62
teeth 16, 18–19, 30, 37, 42, 46, 53–5, 75–6
tummy 13–15, 17, 69

vegetarians 12, 18, 67
Victoria, Queen 68

walking 26–7, 70

"The text bounces from one fascinating fact to the next…" *The Guardian*

"These books … provide a great deal of information in a highly accessible way using a small amount of easily read text imaginatively combined with plenty of line drawings … a good choice for dinosaur fans who are also reluctant readers as well as those who are already enthusiastic." *Wordpool News*